# THE 21 LAWS
# OF
# BEING A BIKINI
# BARISTA

Piper Anne has worked as a bikini barista in the Pacific Northwest for over three years, most of which has been at BlendzGirls in Lacey, Washington. She is a graduate from The Evergreen State College and an entrepreneur.

Darius Allen has a degree in economics from the University of Southern California. He is an author, publisher and the curator of The 21 Laws.

ALSO BY THE 21 LAWS

*The 21 Laws of Surviving a Gentlemen's Club*
*The 21 Laws of Being an Exotic Dancer*
*The 21 Laws of Strip Club Economics*

# THE 21 LAWS
# OF
# BEING A BIKINI
# BARISTA

Piper Anne

A Darius Allen Production

*Varsity Club*

PUBLISHED BY VARSITY CLUB PUBLISHING
a division of Varsity Club Enterprises, LLC.

www.the21laws.com
www.varsityclubinc.com

*Varsity Club*

is a registered trademark of Varsity Club Enterprises, LLC.
Manufactured and printed in the United States of America
Library of Congress Cataloging in Publication Data


The 21 Laws of Being a Bikini Barista/Piper Anne and Darius Allen
1. Coffee & Tea 2. Business & Economics
3. Women's Studies 4. Human Sexuality


ISBN: 978-0-9974320-7-7

Cover design and Illustrations by Jesse Gonzales
Edited by Trojans

# CONTENTS

## LAW 21

# The Barista Note

When you read the words 'bikini barista' it's not the word 'barista' that jumps out. The bikini, by design, is eye-catching, attention-grabbing, and leaves little to the imagination. Be it sling, string, micro, or strapless; each bikini is as captivating and entrancing as the next. As a bikini barista, it's not what you wear that will make you successful; it's how you wear it. The bikini isn't just some cloth and string. It stands for so much more:

**B**old

**I**rresistible

**K**ind

**I**nviting

**N**imble-witted

**I**nfatuating

Now, get ready to make coffee and don't forget your bikini.

# Introduction

Never trust anyone who doesn't drink coffee.

—AJ Lee

When you hear the term 'America's Pastime', you might not think of coffee. Coffee is a lifestyle to some and an addiction to others. It can also be a hobby.

In the Pacific Northwest, coffee has the potential and likelihood of becoming all three. Ever since the introduction of bikini coffee and the bikini barista, the day-to-day experience of getting a cup of coffee has been elevated to anything but mundane.

For the average coffee lover, hearing the terms 'bikini' and 'coffee' together in a sentence is far from the norm, but in Washington State, it's almost as common as rainy days. This unique phenomenon, where it's possible to stop at a drive-thru on the way to work and be served by a friendly, scantily clad barista, makes the coffee that much more stimulating and addictive.

The bikini barista possesses the ability to make a cup of coffee much sweeter and more inviting by mixing the right amount of excellent customer service skills, seemingly effortless sex appeal, and the art of serving the perfect shot of espresso.

As fascinating as they might be, the bikini barista is still elusive to many in mainstream America. With the slow spread of bikini coffee throughout the nation, the ins and outs of the job remain shrouded in mystery. What they do and how they do it is certainly an art form. Because, contrary to public perception, it takes much more than a slingshot bikini to achieve success in the profession.

Navigating the bikini coffee industry, both as a barista and as a thirsty patron, can be intimidating, especially without direction, but it doesn't have to be.

Welcome to The 21 Laws of Being a Bikini Barista.

# THE 21 LAWS
# OF
# BEING A BIKINI
# BARISTA

# LAW
# 1

KNOW YOUR COFFEE AND HOW TO
MAKE IT

*Pouring espresso is an art, one that requires the
barista to care about the quality of the beverage.*

—Howard Schultz

Appearance and sex appeal are essential
factors to being successful as a bikini barista, as is
personality and customer service skills. But none of
which will make your shifts busy or help retain
customers if you cannot make a good cup of coffee.
Espresso is an art, and you need to master it. Being
knowledgeable about your products and how to use

them will get you far as a bikini barista.

Most stands serve more than just dark espresso including white coffee, protein shakes, smoothies, blended coffee beverages, milkshakes, energy drink "spritzers" and food items. Memorizing how to make each drink with accuracy and consistency will take time and lots of practice. Many drinks will start with coffee of some form or another, so it's imperative to know how to actually make it and make it well.

To make good espresso, it is important to understand the anatomy of a shot, how each part of said shot can affect the flavor of a beverage and how to pull a shot. To start the process, you will add grounds to the portafilter, which is a removable part of the espresso machine and where the espresso will pour out of. After adding a small mountain of grounds, tap the portafilter on the counter, then use the tamp to level off the grounds. Hold the portafilter on the counter then press down the grounds with the tamp, applying 20-30 pounds of pressure at a ninety-degree angle, rotating in one direction only. If you do not keep your wrist straight during this, it is possible to give yourself a repetitive motion injury, which you definitely don't want. Repeat the tamping process several times then tip the portafilter upside-down to remove the loose and excess grounds. If you have tamped correctly, the puck of grounds will stay put when the portafilter is inverted. Snap this into your machine, ensuring that it is all the way tightened, then push start and watch your shots pour.

Shots should be in three layers (the heart, the body, and the crema) and should pour between 18 and 23 seconds, however, every espresso machine is different, and color can be more important. If your shots are too dark, they'll taste bitter and this will linger into the taste of the drink, making it less than pleasant to drink. If shots are too light, they're under-extracted and will have a weak and watery flavor. Shots should be golden brown, having a dark heart (the very bottom of the shot), with golden ripples in the body. The very top should be a clearly defined and rich golden crema, adding a sweeter taste to the shots. As the shot settles, the heart will grow to consume the body, leading to more bitterness. Pour your shots quickly and don't let them "expire" or "die." Practice will make perfect and lead to consistency and an excellent espresso every time. Familiarize yourself with your machine and its intricacies and anatomy. Every machine is different and you will develop muscle memory after some time, which will help you pick up speed while still making coffee with consistency.

Once you have mastered the art of standard espresso, it will be time to turn your attention to and understand how to pull shots of white coffee. Simply put, white coffee is coffee that has been roasted for less time, thus preserving caffeine content and resulting in a milder and nutty flavor. Unlike standard espresso, you'll fill the portafilter with white coffee about 3/4 of the way full, then tighten the portafilter into the machine and extract. Do not tamp, and do not serve the first two shots. Instead, discard them and wait ten seconds to allow the white coffee to "steep" and develop flavor. After waiting, you can extract shots again from the same grounds (as long as the portafilter has not been removed during this process). You can do this a total of three times, though you will only serve shots from the last two extractions to ensure your white coffee-based beverages are of utmost quality.

While your shots, standard, white, or decaf, can make or break a drink, knowing how to froth milk and how much syrup or sauce to add to each beverage holds just as much importance. Frothing milk is the process of turning milk into foam. This is done with the steam wand and takes practice to perfect. Start by turning on the steam wand and placing it about half an inch into the milk at a slight angle to create a vortex. As the milk expands, watch your thermometer and stop steaming at around 150 to 155 degrees Fahrenheit. The temperature will continue to rise to a perfect 160 degrees. A cloyingly sweet or flavorless coffee will be unpleasant to drink. Count your syrup pours and your scoops of flavored powders. Every stand has a different amount that they'll add to a beverage. Remember this and you'll have a much easier time preparing coffee quickly and effortlessly. Use precision and consistency and your customers will thank you and be much more inclined to return. You are a barista and should have had adequate training. You have zero excuses to serve bad coffee. Period. Always serve coffee almost as good as the view.

## BARISTA NOTE

Although 'bikini' is the word that jumps out, barista is the word that represents the foundation of the profession. And fundamentally, knowing how to make coffee and make it well is the first step to long-term success in the bikini coffee industry.

# LAW
# 2

YOU ARE YOUR BEST INVESTMENT

*Invest in yourself. Your career is the engine of your wealth.*

—Paul Clitheroe

While the job consists of making and serving delicious coffee, the standards are undoubtedly higher for bikini baristas when it comes to physical appearance in comparison to "regular" baristas. Coffee is an easily acquired commodity in the Pacific Northwest, but bikini-clad women aren't necessarily as easy to come by.

In the bikini coffee industry, appearance *does* matter, and it *can* be costly to maintain; however, it is very worth it. The assumption that a bikini barista arrives at work, removes her clothes, and serves coffee, is far from the truth and it doesn't account for the time and money that is necessary to invest into oneself.

Given that almost all of the body is visible while working as a bikini barista, a much larger surface area has to be taken into account for when getting ready for work.

Being prepared to invest a significant amount of money to maintain your overall appearance and personal brand is something that often goes unspoken about upon hire or during training, yet it is integral to having success and making an impact in the bikini coffee industry. Between the various outfits, the collection of makeup, consistently getting your hair and nails done, keeping a golden tan, and other necessary practices such as hair removal, it's easy to spend hundreds of dollars every month simply getting ready and prepared for work.

The above account doesn't even touch on the cost of lingerie, bikinis and other accessories for work. You will have to spend money to make money in this industry. Do not be naive and assume otherwise.

While the cost of being a bikini barista is frequently underestimated, even more so is the *time* spent making oneself presentable for their jobs. Despite this, many bikini baristas will spend a vast amount of time getting ready for work, sometimes hours, between doing their hair, a full face of makeup, trying on and planning outfits and shaving. It can be tempting to want to skip some of these practices, but at the end of the day, you will only be hurting yourself and your profits. The more you spend, the more you're likely to earn as you'll be more confident and visually appealing to your customers. After all, you aren't just selling coffee. You're selling a fantasy too.

## BARISTA NOTE

You are a brand, and no brand can exist without a significant amount of investment. Be prepared to invest in your brand so you can put yourself in a position to succeed.

# LAW
# 3

ADD AN EXTRA DOSE OF AN EGO
BOOST

*To have a little recognition, that is very nice, you dig. It is good for the ego, for the psyche.*

—Dexter Gordon

Deep down, everyone likes to feel good, important, valued, and attractive. Without a doubt, this includes your customers, who will most likely be men. To make men feel good about themselves, you'll need to know how to boost the male ego with the right amount of sincerity. There are three key concepts that you should keep in mind to make this law much more natural to execute. Adding these concepts together will give an extra dose of an ego boost to your already loyal and new prospective customers.

## A DOSE OF COMPLIMENTS

For starters, the most proven way to make anyone (male or female) feel attractive or desirable is to give genuine compliments. Take the necessary time to find something to compliment each and every customer on, and don't worry if you happen to use the same praise over and over again. The goal is to compliment. Mention their eye color, their adorable smile or how you love their favorite shirt. If they happen to be talking about how many hours they worked, tell them what a hard worker they are and how admirable a trait that is.

That type of recognition would make anyone feel good about themselves, regardless of gender. Positive words and affirmations are contagious, and everyone enjoys being around someone that brings a breath of fresh air to the harshness of ordinary life. And if you're that bikini barista, they'll be back for coffee and a dose of compliments.

## A DOSE OF QUESTIONS

While making small talk several times a day

can be tedious and emotionally exhausting, it's vital to make every single one of your customers feel like the most "fascinating" person on the planet. Do not hesitate to ask them questions about themselves, their job, their families, and if they're from the area.

Do they have pets? What about any unique interests or hobbies?

Never forget that a simple, "How is your day?", said with an open ear, ready to actively listen and participate in the conversation is a compelling gesture that adds to the coffee experience.

It's easy to go into autopilot and respond with a simple, "oh, okay", or "mm-hmm", but you don't want to give the customer the impression that their words are going in one ear and right out the other. Be attentive and ask even more questions and respond thoughtfully. The more meaningful the conversation seems (or is), the more personable you'll be perceived.

## A DOSE OF PERSONALIZATION

Asking engaging questions and exchanging dialogue with customers will not only create a pleasurable customer service experience, but it will also make them more likely to return to your stand. When they do decide to return, it's helpful in the long run if you attempt to memorize something from their previous visit. Rekindle the flame of sorts, and continue the conversation with ease and enthusiasm. Again, ask more questions, but personalize them. Being attentive and completely locked-in will not only impress your customer, but they'll feel that added dose of personalization since you took the time to remember something or another about them personally. The more important and special you make someone feel, the more likely they are to return to see their favorite bikini barista, become a regular and tip generously.

## BARISTA NOTE

Every customer likes to feel appreciated for their time and money spent. And when you add an extra dose of an ego boost, that's the whipped cream on top that makes the coffee experience even sweeter.

# LAW
# 4

DRESS THE PART, BUT KNOW THE
CODE

*The bikini is the most important thing since the
atom bomb.*

—Diana Vreeland

Your work uniform, or dress code, will likely
be imposed by your employer; however, this isn't
always the case. If your employer *does* impose a
dress code, be ready to follow it, be it themed outfits
or certain amounts of coverage. While not all bikini
stands require themed lingerie or costumes, some
do, so be prepared to purchase these items. If

required, then get creative. Variety is the spice of life and utilizing it will make you stand out.

Themes can be highly specific, such as wearing pink on Wednesdays or fishnets on Fridays. While this can make getting ready and planning for your shift more simple and fun, keep in mind that it can also be a huge financial investment. Lingerie isn't cheap. If your stand imposes themes, it's likely that they'll impose said dress code rules to prevent the possibility of violating any public nudity laws. Many bikini barista stands don't mandate what their bikini baristas wear, but the ones that do will likely require you to wear either pasties, a thong, or both every day. Some can even be as strict as to dictate what type of shoes you wear on each day of the week.

If you're lucky enough to work at a stand that doesn't impose any dress code or uniform requirements, it is still important to thoroughly read and comprehend the public nudity laws in the particular area of business. It's only smart that you protect yourself from legal consequences such as public nudity charges (a misdemeanor offense), tickets or fines, and possibly an arrest. Compliance with the law will significantly reduce or eliminate the risk of any violation.

Nudity laws can and will vary, not only from county to county but from city to city as well. They can be as liberal as allowing body paint or fishnets without pasties, or as strict as prohibiting underboob and side-boob. While your employer should, and likely will inform you of these limitations, you should take the initiative to search and review these in order to fully understand your rights. Again, it's crucial that you comply with these laws but do so creatively and with savviness. It is possible to wear much more than a bikini in areas where full bikini coverage is required.

## BARISTA NOTE

Putting the 'bikini' in bikini barista sounds like an easy job, but more often than not, there is a dress code enforced. Knowing what you can wear and what not to wear is vital to keeping your job and growing your customer base.

# LAW
# 5

SET CLEAR BOUNDARIES WITH
CUSTOMERS

*Boundary setting is really a huge part of time
management.*

—Jim Loehr

As you develop closer relationships with
your customers, it's important to set clear
boundaries. Doing so respectfully and with tact will
help prevent any uncomfortable situations from
arising. It will also prevent customers from taking
advantage of you or having false assumptions of
what is and isn't okay. Regardless of how skimpy

your bikini, you still have the right to be treated with respect by customers and it's more than acceptable to stand up for yourself in certain situations.

Many customers will assume that because you're nice to them (even though you're paid to do so), you have some personal interest in them. While it behooves you to feign interest, it is equally important to know how to turn someone down without offending, embarrassing, or making them feel bad which could prevent them from returning. Regardless of your marital or relationship status or sexual orientation, it isn't recommended to let a customer know that you're taken or not interested in men (or women, depending on the customer). Part of what a bikini barista sells is the illusion of availability. You want customers to think they have a chance with you. It'll keep them interested and coming back for more.

## CAN I GET YOUR NUMBER?

If and when a customer asks for your number, there are several ways to say no (which is highly recommended) politely. It is very easy to say that you don't give out personal information due to safety purposes. Even easier to say that it's against company policy and another barista recently got in trouble for that same action. Yes, that is going to be a lie, but it removes responsibility from you and places it on your employer who honestly probably doesn't actually care what you do with your phone number.

## WANNA GO OUT SOMETIME?

If asked on a date, it's equally as simple to decline politely. You're either too busy, or it's against company policy to date customers. You can also say you'll think about it, but conveniently forget to until they remind you when they see you next time.

It is okay to say no, and you probably should.

## CAN I SEE THE REST?

Saying no when customers ask to be flashed or "for a show" can be a little trickier. That request happens more often than one would think and it's not legal. Politely remind your customer that you don't want a ticket for public nudity, and the cameras at the stand see everything. You don't want to jeopardize your job for their quick thrill. Some baristas do or have given shows, but that doesn't mean you have to. If a customer mentions that, you can say, "Sorry, I don't do that", and continue to give them excellent customer service. If a customer doesn't respect when you say 'no', remember that you have the right to refuse service.

## HOW MUCH FOR A PICTURE?

Sometimes you'll find the occasional customer that would like to take pictures of you. Depending on how you feel about this, you can 100% always say no. Remember that you don't know where these pictures will end up. If you're unbothered by this, by all means charge for photos and secure the bag. Between five and ten dollars is pretty commonplace, and that should be per photo. Don't sell yourself short if you decide to allow customers to take photos of you. Unfortunately, you might encounter someone who tries to take photos of you without your consent. If this occurs, try to remain calm and ask them to stop and delete the photos or videos. Remind them that no one likes to be photographed or recorded without express permission.

While those customers that try to photograph without consent can be annoying, don't be surprised if some customers non-consensually expose their genitals to you. Sadly, it happens, albeit infrequently, but when it does, you're left feeling violated and uncomfortable. Immediately let the customer know that exposing themselves in such a manner is a sexual offense, and then smile because they're on camera and you'll be notifying the police. *Your employer should have security cameras; and if they don't, the customer does not under any circumstances need to know.*

If you ask the customer to leave, make sure to get their vehicle type and license plate number, then inform your boss/manager and call the police. While they might not be able to do much, it can offer peace of mind that they most likely won't be returning.

Another less conventional way to handle this would be to tell them they can add a zero to their tip or you'll contact the police or local authorities. Whatever you choose to do, don't just ignore it or the same customers will return and likely continue to expose themselves to you.

You do not have to tolerate disgusting behavior, and this is NOT part of your job description. Neither is tolerating or partaking in dirty talk. Regardless of what a customer is doing or asking of you, set clear boundaries and speak up if they make you feel uncomfortable in any way. You are paid to be nice to customers, not to take sh*t from them.

## BARISTA NOTE

There's a thin line between excellent customer service and being at someone's service. Setting clear boundaries will notify customers that you're at work to make coffee, not to mix business and pleasure.

# LAW
# 6

## SUCCESS IS IN THE DETAILS

*Success in any endeavor requires single-minded attention to detail and total concentration.*

—Willie Sutton

In an industry with lots of competition, you'll need every advantage you can gather to not only succeed and stay above water but to stand out and make a lasting impact. It's true that you can be the prettiest, the fastest, and the most masterful at making coffee, but none of this will matter if you don't have an eye for detail. Adhering to this law is the edge that you *will* need if you want to be the best in the business. The type of edge that will keep your customers coming back for more and more. You will need to see the bigger picture while simultaneously realizing that it's comprised of seemingly minute and insignificant details. Perfect that skill and understand that outlook and you will succeed.

This law is all about going that extra mile, inch by inch. Whether or not a customer becomes your regular (which is the ultimate goal) hinges on every interaction you have with them.

Your first impression happens as soon as the customer pulls up. Always open a window and greet a customer immediately; never close that window until they leave, regardless of how cold it is or what the weather is like. Consider inclement weather an occupational hazard.

If you're serving someone else, let them know you'll be right with them, otherwise, always greet a customer and ask how they're doing before taking their order. You want to be personable. Unfortunately, you're not an oracle and many customers don't know what they want to drink. Be prepared to narrow it down through a process of elimination; ask what they do and don't like, and have ideas ready and recipes memorized. Offer a special if your stand has one. Make the beverage before you tell them what it is as sometimes something sounds a lot worse than it actually is, especially as you get more creative. *Always* offer to remake a drink if the customer doesn't like it, and tell them you'll gladly do so regardless of how much experience you have in making coffee. Even the act of letting them know your willingness to do so invites the customer to be more honest with you and makes them feel as if you *actually* care about them. Which you do, of course.

When a customer knows what they like to drink but doesn't give enough detail, make sure to avoid asking question after question. No one likes to feel interrogated. The easiest way to avoid this is to lump questions together. Instead of asking what size of beverage the customer wants then asking how many shots they want, ask what size and how many shots they'd like as one question instead of two. This will give you more time to ask them more personal questions, like how their day went, what they're doing this weekend, etc. Seem genuinely interested, even if you're not.

The subtleties of how you serve coffee and interact with the customer can vary depending on the number of people in the vehicle and what gender or age they are. Always make drinks for children at a much cooler temp (around 120 degrees, maximum), and offer whipped cream, sprinkles, and suckers. Whisper about that though because not every parent wants their children to have those items, and if the child overhears it, they'll probably be upset if their parent says no. Be discrete. Never hand over an iced coffee if the bottom is still warm. Always give women their drinks first and address them directly while making eye contact, especially if they aren't driving. Try to interact with *every* customer, especially if there's multiple in the car. If your car consists of some non-human visitors, offer dog treats and ask permission before doing so. Acknowledging everyone makes the bikini coffee experience that much more personal and special. Not only does this make for an even more memorable experience for everyone, it makes the customers more likely to return.

Every now and then, you will encounter patrons who did not realize that the stand you're working on is a bikini stand. How you handle these cases is extremely important. Be polite (as you should with *every* customer). If the driver seems extremely taken aback, offer to put a robe on to make them more comfortable and try not to lose the sale. Sometimes a customer will deny this and choose to leave. Do not take this personally or be offended. Remember that you are part of a niche market and that you're not everyone's cup of tea (or coffee).

Continue to give everyone the best customer service possible, then try to take a step beyond that: try to memorize faces, names, and drink orders, especially of those you serve frequently. As insignificant as it seems, they will notice and will be much more likely to return. The entire goal in the bikini coffee industry is to make money (we don't just do this for fun). Pay attention. It'll pay off.

# BARISTA NOTE

To find success in the profession, you must always focus on the details. It's the little things that make up an excellent bikini coffee experience and customers never forget the little things.

# LAW
# 7

PLAY NICE: DEALING WITH YOUR
CO-WORKERS

*Establish and maintain good working relationships
with co-workers. You don't have to be friends, but
you do have to be friendly.*

—Judy Smith

More often than not, one bikini barista will
be working at a time. On busier days of the week,
two bikini baristas might be on shift together,
serving coffee at the same time.

However, working solo doesn't necessarily
mean it isn't necessary to develop positive

relationships with your co-workers or exempt you from acting as a team player. You will see your co-workers at the end of a shift and when covering each other's shifts. The better your relationship with your co-workers, the more positive your work environment will be.

Tension and competition will be ever-present in any workforce comprised of hardworking individuals. In the bikini coffee industry, it's easier to avoid confrontation as most shifts are solo, yet this doesn't mean that friction and disputes don't find a way to your stand. While a multitude of things can cause tension between baristas, most commonly, it can be attributed to shift changes and closes, and frivolous gossip.

Both issues are easily avoidable.

## IT'S YOUR DUTY TO DO YOUR DUTIES

Simply completing all your duties on shift change and closing can reduce tension between you and your co-workers. The pressure of coming on shift and having to clean up after another barista is not only discouraging but frustrating. No one wants to feel as if they're doing someone else's job for them. You're a bikini barista, not a bikini maid or bikini babysitter. While closing duties are much more extensive, it is imperative to do a complete restock and thorough cleaning of the stand. An excellent rule of thumb for both of these transitions is to leave the stand how you would like to find it—clean and presentable.

## IT'S BETTER TO BE THE BIGGER PERSON

Interacting with your co-workers positively and with kindness will also play a role in how you'll get along and maintain a peaceful working environment. While this in and of itself is integral to your relationships, your indirect actions will also cause a negative impact. Although it's easy to gripe and complain about irresponsible co-workers, particularly if they leave the stand dirty or understocked for your shift, it is unprofessional, and it will get back to them and reflect negatively on both of you.

Customers also tend to pass along whatever sentiments you mention in regards to others, so speak with kindness and compliments, even if it's an exaggeration of the truth. As far as you know, all of your co-workers are nice girls and you "love to work with them."

Your other co-workers don't necessarily need to know how much one of your fellow employees annoys you and gets on your last nerve. Triangulation and passive aggressive behavior won't get you far or benefit you at all. If you happen to be the recipient of catty behavior, be the bigger person and keep looking at the bigger picture.

Retaliation with slander or not completing

your work duties will only exacerbate any tensions that might arise. A positive work environment is much more suitable to work in and it begins with girls you'll see, albeit in passing, every day. Be nice; no one likes a mean girl.

## BARISTA NOTE

Although you'll mainly be solo on the job, it's still vital that you maintain cordial working relationships with your fellow bikini baristas. A positive environment is a reflection of you and your work ethic.

# LAW
# 8

SAFETY FIRST, SAFETY LAST

*At the end of the day, the goals are simple: safety and security.*

—Jodi Rell

Bikini baristas are in an inherently vulnerable position: working alone, in scantily clad outfits, sometimes in secluded areas and at weird times of the day/night. It is no surprise that safety is of concern to both employers and baristas alike. Knowing how to keep yourself safe while on shift will pay off in the industry and help prevent any potentially dangerous situations as well as give yourself peace of mind.

One of the biggest risks associated with working in the bikini coffee industry is the known visibility and reputation for having a high volume of sales. Unfortunately, that type of success brings some unwanted attention and robberies have been known to occur at bikini stands.

If you've worked in any sales position before, you've likely received training on what to do in case of a robbery: #1 be compliant. Your life isn't worth any amount of money, and you shouldn't face any backlash from your employer in this case.

If you do, it's time to find another stand.

While there is little you can do in case of a robbery, there are things you can do to safeguard yourself from potential bodily harm. Most bikini stands are equipped with alarm systems and some with panic buttons. Familiarize yourself with the location of both of these and how they work.

In addition, there will likely be mace or some other form of self-defense mechanism at the stand. Know how to use those items and maybe consider investing in a small knife for yourself. If you work opening or closing shifts, you'll be walking alone to and from your car (in the dark, depending on the time of year). You must always be aware of your surroundings in and outside the stand.

Your employer might (and should) offer at least basic training and guidelines for what to do in various situations. They might also enforce policies/ protocol in regards to this as well. Using common sense will be invaluable on the off chance that they don't. Walk-up customers can also be dangerous as they are much more easily able to reach out and grab you or your tip jar. *Remember that you have the right to refuse service to anyone and do NOT serve walk-ups when it is dark.* If you do experience or notice a suspicious customer (or are made to feel uncomfortable), trust your instincts. Do not hesitate to call the police in emergencies. There are certain risks not worth taking, and those involving your wellbeing fall under that category.

Safety involves much more than what can happen outside the stand. Being smart when it comes to working with scalding liquids with little to no protection from clothing can create a whole different set of problems. Customers will ask all the time if you burn yourself. You shouldn't if you're aware of your body and immediate surroundings. If spilling a hot drink (it *will* happen), do not under any circumstances attempt to catch it. Instead, jump backwards or out of the way as quickly as possible. It is easier to clean a beverage off the floor than to endure a first or second-degree burn. Steam wands produce—you guessed it, steam, which is typically very hot. Avoid turning this on unless its in liquids or if a rag is over the end, as steam can burn you just as severely as hot liquids. But burns aren't the only thing you'll need to be wary of when working as a bikini barista. If you're wearing heels (which you probably will be), you're at an increased risk of slipping. Again, maintain environmental awareness and sweep up any ice you might drop or wipe up spills. The last thing you want to do is injure yourself on shift.

While an employer might have safeguards or security systems in place to ensure your safety, it is ultimately your responsibility. Be self-aware and equally aware of your surroundings. Trust your instincts and stay vigilant. The bikini coffee industry has risks like any other and isn't inherently dangerous. Prioritize your safety and you shouldn't have any problems.

## BARISTA NOTE

There's nothing more important than your safety. Before you can even think about being the best bikini barista, your wellbeing and overall sanity must first be in a healthy space so you can perform at a high level.

# LAW
# 9

THE BEST PROMOTION IS SELF-
PROMOTION

*Many of us have this mind-set which considers self-promotion a taboo.*

—Abhishek Ratna

The best way to make money as a bikini barista is to have busy shifts. To accomplish this, you'll want to promote your shifts and schedule to new and old customers alike. Don't hesitate to do so or be shy about this. You are your number one marketing tool. It is important to know how to maximize traffic to your stand, so utilize social media as an advantage and brand yourself as one of the best.

The easiest way to let customers know where you'll be and when is in person. If you're new, in general, or new to a stand, this is the opportune moment to share your schedule over and over without seeming too pushy. If customers ask when you'll be back, which they should if you give them excellent service, offer to write your schedule down for them and include any social media you use to market with. It'll make you more accessible and they're less likely to forget your schedule. At the end of every transaction, tell a customer that you'll see them tomorrow (if you work the following day), or whenever your next shift is. It's more specific than "see you soon", without being overly assertive.

You can only advertise so much in person, so it will be to your advantage to consider utilizing social media to draw in customers, especially those that might be completely unaware of your existence (remember: we all start somewhere). In the bikini coffee industry, Instagram is the most popular platform to promote stands and shifts alike. Your employer might run an Instagram page for the stand and require you to either post pictures there directly or send in pictures to be posted. Not all stands use this marketing tool, but it is something to keep in mind when entering the industry, especially if you're trying to maintain anonymity for any multitude of reasons. Consider leaving any recognizable details out of photos and/or using a stage name if this is a concern. Get creative here and remember that this is where you will ultimately end up branding yourself.

If you do go the route of starting your own bikini barista Instagram page, always let your customers know about it and tell them they can follow you to see when you're working and what you're wearing. Understand that this is another time commitment that will be of little benefit to you if you're inconsistent. Post frequently and be interactive with your fans and followers, giving them updates on any schedule (or stand) changes. Building a following does take time but the more dedicated you are, the more beneficial it will be to you, particularly when it comes to enticing new customers to visit you.

It should be noted that Instagram has some community guidelines that aren't necessarily bikini barista friendly. Be wary when you post to ensure that your account doesn't get disabled, which has been happening throughout the industry with increasing frequency. To circumvent this, some baristas have opted to use Twitter as their primary marketing tool instead. Their content policy is much more lax, however, Twitter is one of the social media platforms with the slowest account growth. This doesn't necessarily mean it isn't worth doing. Sometimes the best things take time. Marketing is still marketing regardless of how or where it's done, and you'll need to do it in order to be successful.

## BARISTA NOTE

If you don't promote yourself as a bikini barista, who else will? You have to be your own #1 fan. Get creative, self-promote and grow your following.

# LAW
# 10

## ALWAYS KEEP A CLEAN
## WORKSPACE

*I look forward to spring cleaning and putting things
in their place. It's therapeutic for me.*

—Kimora Lee Simmons

To be *any* kind of barista, you'll need to
acquire a food handlers' permit. This acquisition
should be a no-brainer and it further enhances the
importance of having a clean and sanitary work
environment. When you complete the training
required for this certification, you'll need to adhere
to all of these requirements strictly. Otherwise, your

stand could get citations and/or shut down, resulting in the loss of your job.

There is a common misconception that because bikini baristas are wearing less clothes and they present a free-spirited attitude, the coffee stand will be "dirty" or unhygienic. Utilizing food safety habits is necessary in the bikini coffee industry for more than one reason, and negating this stigma is one of them. .

Maintaining a clean workspace will be beneficial to you in many ways. If you were to drive to a coffee stand and notice that the barista (clothed or otherwise) had a dirty workspace or filthy hands, you would probably be wary about the drink you were about to be served. If your stand looks sloppy and unpresentable, your customers will have the same view of the beverage and the quality of service —unprofessional.

An unkempt stand will also add a lot of visual clutter that might not be noticeable, but it will register subconsciously, be it a dirty floor or counters, to piles of coffee grounds or dirty shot glasses. You don't want anything to distract customers from you or the experience you're selling. Furthermore, it is simply unsanitary to allow your stand to become a complete mess. If you're not regularly wiping your counters down, rinsing your milk pitchers, or washing your hands, you're just spreading germs and reinforcing the idea that bikini stands aren't hygienic or professional.

When it comes to hygiene standards, which should be clearly outlined by your food handlers' training and general training, they will likely include a multitude of "chores" that aren't optional. These include but not limited to disinfecting surfaces, properly cleaning an espresso machine, and regularly checking expiry dates of perishable products.

While shift change and closing duties can vary, it's safe to assume that all dishes, blenders, and utensils should be washed every night. As tempting as it might be to cut corners in this area, you'll only be hurting yourself, your co-workers who have to follow you on shift, and your stand that has to undergo health inspections regularly. Be a bikini barista but don't be *that* bikini barista.

## BARISTA NOTE

Presenting a clean workspace is the best first impression that you and your stand can give. It represents the level of professionalism, dedication, and quality of service and products offered.

# LAW
# 11

UNDERSTAND THE MARKET AND
BE AWARE OF LOCAL
COMPETITION

*It is nice to have valid competition; it pushes you to
do better.*

—Gianni Versace

As bikini coffee is ubiquitous in the Pacific
Northwest (even more specifically Washington
State), the abundance of bikini coffee stands leads to
plenty of competition due to the sheer volume of
bikini baristas. Understanding how this can affect

you as a current or hopeful bikini barista will benefit you during the job hunt process as well as in the long-term.

When starting your career as a bikini barista, be discerning when applying to stands. While it is hard to know which stands are busy or not without already being a part of the industry, the adage that location is everything holds true. Look for bikini stands in busier areas. The greater the population, the more potential customers. Some might not be the most accessible depending on where you live, but stands in metropolitan areas tend to have more traffic than ones in more rural areas. Don't let this be the sole deciding factor in where you apply.

Due to market oversaturation, look for stands that have been in business for a while. Their staying power is indicative of the fact that business has been steady and consistent for years, which means you have a higher earning potential. More time = more regulars = busier location (this will be very important to keep in mind). Note the number of stands in a certain area. This observation will typically mean several things: the area is busy for bikini coffee, there is more competition between stands and baristas, and business will be split up between stands. Keep all of this in mind when choosing your bikini coffee home.

To be competitive, you'll want to build a regular clientele base. Utilize your skills in sales, customer service, and, of course, be *that bikini barista.* Once you have your regulars, continuing to be your best will be integral in keeping them loyal and from "cheating" on you with other stands and baristas. Stand rivalry does exist in the industry, so be prepared to work hard, especially when getting settled in at a new stand.

Keep in mind that relocating to a rival stand and/or stand hopping can not only earn you a reputation as a poor barista, but it will make it more difficult for your loyal patrons to follow and continue to visit you. Unless serious issues arise at your workplace, try to stay put and build your brand with stability. The longer you remain at one stand, the greater the number of customers will become familiarized with you. Brand recognition will make your shifts infinitely busier, thus exponentially more profitable for you. Building regulars can take time, especially in a highly competitive industry with hundreds of baristas and potential baristas waiting to put their bikinis on. Don't be discouraged; just keep an edge, be consistent, and always keep an eye on your competition.

# BARISTA NOTE

When it comes to the Pacific Northwest, you'll never be the only bikini barista in town. The bikini coffee industry is competitive and the market is ever-growing. To compete, you must always stay learning and ready to make a name for yourself.

# LAW
# 12

MANAGE EXPECTATIONS: THE
TOPIC OF TIPS

*Don't stare at our tips unless you tit us.*

—Anonymous

Few baristas go into the bikini coffee
industry simply because they love making coffee and
being nude. It's understood that the income,
primarily in the form of tipping, is what draws girls
in. You will more than likely make minimum wage
(at least in Washington State), but tips will make up
the majority of your income. These are not
guaranteed, and it is important to understand that

your income is variable and not fixed. Feeling entitled to a tip will not only disappoint you when some days are better than others (and they will be), but it could lead to resentment if a customer doesn't tip (and some won't).

It's an unspoken understanding that you're working for tips, so it's important not to let the customer know that in a more indirect than direct sense. Regardless of whether they tip or not, make sure to give the customer the same excellent service. If someone doesn't tip you, definitely do not ask them to, or ask for a higher tip, or complain about the lack of tips. Again, you're not entitled to their tip and acting as such can be offensive, especially if a customer thinks you only want their money instead of their company. Whatever tip you do receive should be accepted with extreme gratitude. Comment on the customer's generosity (with sincerity) even if they just give you a handful of change.

Continuing with the idea that a customer should remain oblivious to the idea that your primary goal is to earn tips, there are several small yet very important things you must do and must never do. These subtleties are seemingly insignificant but are extremely noticeable when disregarded. You will look presumptuous if you reach into a tip jar or exchange tips out in the till in front of a customer. Regularly empty your tip jars, but never in front of a customer. Make sure to keep the tips you have inside, out of the line of your customers' vision. They do not need to know how much you make. Some will ask and the best answer is to say that tips vary and it's similar to waitressing. It isn't a lie, but it's not a specific answer, which frankly isn't any of their business.

While your tips do vary from shift to shift, they can and will vary from the time of day, to the day of the week, to the month and season. Despite all of these variables, the amount you make in tips can serve as a sort of litmus tests indicative of the quality of your customer service. Aim to earn the equivalent of thirty to fifty percent of your coffee sales in tips. It is great to set goals such as these and rewarding to achieve them, but remember, it is never a guarantee, so stay humble and gracious.

## BARISTA NOTE

When it comes to tips, they are supposed to be welcomed, and appreciated, but never expected. Focus on providing the best bikini coffee experience, and your tips will start to add up.

# LAW
# 13

BE READY TO GET READY

*So if you stay ready, you ain't gotta get ready, and that is how I run my life.*

—Will Smith

You may or may not be one of the lucky girls that wake up looking refreshed. Not everyone is, but the standards of what is considered as "being ready" for work in the bikini coffee industry are significantly higher than most customer service industries. Know how to get ready for work, actually do it, and do it well.

While it is important to note that a bikini barista has to do more than simply look the part, she still has to look the part. With her whole body on display, there is a lot of surface area to cover, especially since most of it is uncovered. Getting ready for work and being presentable in the bikini coffee industry has many steps, and it starts with basic hygiene. No amount of makeup or hairspray can replace that. Shower and shave regularly. No, customers will not be touching you, but body hair is visible and body odor can waft. Keep a razor and deodorant in your work bag. Better yet, keep a toothbrush there too. Poor oral hygiene is a turn-off in any industry, so maintaining yourself isn't optional, especially when you need to be oozing sex appeal.

Once basic cleanliness is achieved, it is important to understand the expectations of what your physical appearance is being held to. Wearing makeup is a requirement, not a recommendation. This doesn't mean that you need to be full glam every day. At the very least, remember the Eyes & Lips rule (which is the bare minimum): always have something on your eyes and lips, which can be as simple as mascara and lip gloss. It will help you look more put together than having a bare face at work. When getting ready for work, it is important to do this *at home*. You wouldn't apply makeup on shift at almost any other job, which makes it unacceptable to do it as a bikini barista.

Makeup is important, but it isn't the only thing you will need to do to get ready for work.

Whether you have short, long, straight, wavy, or curly hair, you have to do *something* with it. Messy buns aren't recommended and neither is bed head. That doesn't mean that you're obligated to curl, straighten, or even wear your hair down every day. Get creative and be receptive to what your customers like (hint: pigtails and braids seem to be pretty popular). At the very least, brush it.

Whatever you decide to do with your hair and however you decide to do your makeup, give yourself ample time to do so. If this means waking up and starting to get ready two hours before your shift, then do it. It's important to arrive ready and this time spent can help you mentally prepare for your shift as well. Your first customers should see the same barista as your last customers, even if your shift starts at four-thirty in the morning. Be ready for work before you get to work.

## BARISTA NOTE

As a bikini barista, getting ready for work takes on a different meaning, especially compared to 'regular' baristas. You have to be ready to look the part, and then get ready to play the part.

# LAW
# 14

## UNDERSTAND YOUR POSITION:
## SALES, SALES, SALES

*We have a relationship with our customer, and that
relationship translates into sales.*

—Richard Hayne

   Looking the part and being able to make
coffee are just two facets of being a bikini barista.
This is a customer service position and a *sales*
position. You will need to understand how your
sales can make or break your longevity and success
as a bikini barista as well as how to maximize those
sales.

Viewing this position from an employers' perspective will give you a significant amount of insight. Not only will stands be likely to hire outgoing, good looking, and well-spoken girls, but they're also looking for something else that will benefit *them*: motivation and drive. With how numerous bikini coffee stands are in the Pacific Northwest, employers want baristas who can sell coffee and bring in steady traffic. They're looking for peak profits and your sales and regulars are integral to that. Your performance has a direct impact on your job security: you will be replaced if you cannot keep up or if your employers lose money while having you on shift. Your work schedule will also be directly impacted by your ability or inability to bring in customers. Baristas with the most desirable shifts and schedules (typically mornings, Monday through Friday), more often than not, will have the highest sales. This is a direct result of customer service skills, experience, readiness, and drive. It is okay to feel slightly competitive and always strive to be your best. Your stand might impose sales goals; try your hardest to achieve them. If they don't, set your own and kick some ass.

The easiest ways to boost your sales (aside from having a high volume of customers) is to utilize a series of semantic tricks. Up-selling can be as simple as offering extra shots or subtly pushing more expensive flavors or chocolates. You *never* want a customer to feel like you're pushing them, though.

Use the phrase "just". It subconsciously makes them think they can have (and want) more. "Just two shots in that today?". It might make them feel as if that isn't enough and they'll be more inclined to say, "f—k it, add a third." Give the customer options under the guise that the items are on the same price tier (and only in a few instances tell them the price of the add on). Offering milk, white, or dark chocolate can increase your sales as two of those options typically cost more. Tell them which is your favorite, or offer between two name brands: Hershey's vs. Ghirardelli. The customer will usually pick the more appealing of the two (or three). Do they want a drink that is hot, iced, or blended? Blended drinks almost always cost significantly more.

Understanding the products you sell will greatly benefit you, as will having a full and well-versed comprehension of the menu. If a customer asks for an Italian soda, ask if they'd like a Red Bull in that, then ask if they'd like a single (one can) or a double (two cans). Offering extras such as multiple flavors, cream, juice, or real fruit can greatly boost sales. Every cent adds up and can secure shifts, promotions or raises, and your job.

Some stands charge more than others, so be prepared to sell higher costing drinks without guilt. Ring up all add-ons, even if it means your drinks cost much more. There's no point in upselling if you're not going to be utilizing it to the max.

However, it is never okay to overcharge. This is dishonest and will make customers less likely to visit you if your drinks are consistently higher than other baristas. Everyone loves consistency. If a customer seems upset that a drink total is too high, it is easy to pass along this responsibility to your employers (who actually *do* set the prices). Remind them that you only make the coffee and not the prices.

While all of these methods are great ways to boost sales, the best way is to draw in more customers and keep regulars. The higher the volume, the higher the sales, and the higher the more likely you'll be to keep your job and maximize your tips.

## BARISTA NOTE

A major part of your job is to sell a fantasy, a unique coffee experience, but none of that matters if you don't make any sales at the window. Business is about sales, sales, and even more sales.

# LAW
# 15

YOU CAN NEVER HAVE TOO MANY
OUTFITS

*I have too many clothes, I have too many options.*

—Rihanna

Consistency can make or break your success as a bikini barista, however, this does not give you license to be boring. You'll need to captivate customers in order to retain them as regulars. One of the best ways to do this is through your outfits: make sure they fit well and include some variety.

Variety is the spice of life. If you work at a stand that imposes a dress code in the way of themes, much of the creative planning of being a bikini barista has been taken care of. This doesn't mean that you can wear the same outfit for each theme because then you will become predictable and less intriguing. Themes are great but you need to make sure you have several outfits for each theme. One or two will not cut it. Buying accessories can get very expensive very quickly, but it is possible to DIY parts of your outfit with scissors and a hot glue gun. Again, get creative. You don't always need to be this extra, but being basic is not an option. Put in effort; your customers will notice and wonder what you're going to do next.

If you don't work at a stand that requires themed uniforms, then you'll have to be conscientious and not get stuck in a rut of wearing the same outfit or types of outfits day in and day out (be it lace body suits or micro bikinis). Prior planning can help you prevent this by making sure you don't wear the same color or style over and over. It helps to have a general idea of what you're wearing for your next shift. and keep a backup outfit with you in case of spills, rips, tears, or any other wardrobe malfunctions that can (and will) arise. While it is easy to simply wear bikinis every day, it can be visually boring. Try to mix things up and be perceptive of how your customers react to your outfits, then give them more of what they want but with variation.

Regardless of what you choose to wear,

you'll need to wear it well. Try. On. Everything. Before. You. Get. To. Work. (At least once.). Never do a dry run, especially when it comes to boxed sets. The outfit could end up fitting poorly and/or being extremely uncomfortable. You will not feel as confident wearing something that doesn't make you feel sexy.

You will also lose confidence if you're in pain: shoes can easily make or break an outfit. It is highly inadvisable to attempt to break in new boots or shoes at work. If you're getting blisters, it will be difficult to be positive and energetic for your customers, as well as very uncomfortable to be on your feet all day. Wear comfortable shoes, but don't compromise your entire outfit wearing something that isn't cohesive. Sneakers don't go well with lacy lingerie, nor do UGGs or slippers. Even if you don't think customers can see your feet, it will still clash with your overall look. It might not be verbalized, but the juxtaposition will register subconsciously with the customer and something will seem off, even if they can't exactly pinpoint it. This comes back to having an eye for detail in order to be as successful as possible. You might not realize just how important even the most minute of details can be.

While your outfit is important, you'll need to consider other "adornments", per se, that can add that little bit of something extra to any outfit. Accessorize to compliment what you're wearing: thigh-high stockings/socks, a baseball cap, costume jewelry. Even your manicure will be noticed as you hand the customers their drink, so be sure it isn't chipped. Make sure you smell nice, but not overly perfumey (smell is 90% of taste, so you don't want that lingering on their cup). Simply put, the more effort you put in, the more put together you'll look, which can only benefit you. Remember, you're trying to keep your customers guessing and interested. Don't fall into the trap of wearing the same thing over and over. Mix it up.

## BARISTA NOTE

Nothing keeps a customer more intrigued than a wide variety of eye-catching outfits that trigger the imagination. Keeping things fun and unpredictable will always have customers stopping by to see what you have on.

# LAW
# 16

WORK SMARTER, NOT HARDER

*Work smart. Get things done.*

—Susan Wojcicki

Being a bikini barista includes a multitude of job requirements, ranging from maintaining a near perfect appearance, providing customer service second to none, and keeping a *very* clean stand. The combination of all of these things can be overwhelming when coupled with the mental preparation that goes into being successful in the bikini coffee industry. Knowing how to work as efficiently as possible will save you both time and effort as well as serving the highest volume of customers possible in the shortest amount of time. This will, in turn, maximize your earning potential.

Your customers should view you as the barista worth waiting for, however, it's best if you don't keep them waiting for too long. Understanding the process and timing when it comes to making coffee will greatly reduce your wait times (and keep your customers happy!).

Steaming the milk takes the longest, so start it before anything else (unless the drink is iced/blended). Shots come next because they have around 20 seconds until they hit perfection/completion. While you wait for both of those to be ready, there's no reason you can't ring up the beverage or, if you see a regular customer who's drink you've memorized (hint, hint) next in line, start theirs. Starting with whatever takes the longest and working your way down towards more instantaneous tasks such as measuring/scooping powder or stirring will drastically reduce the time spent on each beverage. This kind of efficiency will be invaluable. No one likes to wait and you don't want to feel too pressured working in a fast-paced environment because you feel unable to keep up. Speed comes with practice, so don't feel discouraged, just push yourself to move more quickly. Soon it will come to you naturally.

Practice can only do so much and making coffee isn't your only job responsibility. Being efficient when navigating your work space will prove to be crucial. Simplify your job by restocking and cleaning as your shift progresses. You're only hurting yourself by putting this off as you'll have to stay later during closing or shift change to play catch up. As tempting as it is to simply relax between waves of customers (and yes, they come in waves), it can and likely will slow you down in the long run. You want to work smarter, not harder, so stay on top of things as you go.

## BARISTA NOTE

Knowing how to be efficient and decisive with your duties is important. It will save you time and effort; both needed to meet a heavy demand of customers that want quick and steady service.

# LAW
# 17

USE YOUR SEX APPEAL TO
CAPTIVATE YOUR CUSTOMER

*Sex appeal is fifty percent what you've got and fifty
percent what people think you've got.*

—Sophia Loren

Sex sells. The bikini coffee industry blurs the
line between "regular" coffee and sex work by
utilizing this statement of fact. People are drawn to
bikini stands because the baristas have sex appeal,
and know how to use it. A bikini barista must be
sexy, fun, and alluring in order to draw in traffic.
The bikini coffee experience is like none other and

the baristas are in charge of selling the illusion and experience. You must know exactly how to play any situation to keep your customers thirsty and coming back for more.

You have the ability to be captivating, whether it feels like it or not. Confidence isn't always something you're born with, but it is something you can learn and acquire. As a bikini barista, you are immersed into a world where your body is visible to others and you cannot be shy about it. Introverted or otherwise, you have to play the part. That means faking it until you make it. If you seem shy or insecure, customers will pick up on that and you'll lose some of your appeal.

Everyone loves a confident woman.

Be that woman and let them know you're *that* woman by holding conversation, eye contact, and knowing just how much to flirt.

There's a fine line between being flirtatious and being vulgar. You don't need to dirty talk or make innuendos with every (or even most) customer(s). Instead, subtle hints will go much further. Leave some mystery because mysteriousness can equate to sexiness. If you aren't overly explicit at first, your customers will definitely use their imagination and definitely return for more out of both curiosity and excitement.

Give them a sexy shot of <u>espresso</u> and let them create their idea of you and play along. You want to be:

**E**nticing
**S**weet
**P**rovocative
**R**adiant
**E**ye-catching
**S**ubtle
**S**exy
**O**pen-minded

This shot has everything necessary to captivate a customer.

Understand that a mental image is one thing, but a physical image is another. It is important to leave something to the imagination here as well. Don't show the customer *everything*, but tease them with the possibility that you might. Not only will this drive them crazy, but it'll make them much more likely to visit you with increasing frequency in hopes that they might see something extra. Everyone loves a tease, so master the art of teasing and have fun with it.

Seduction doesn't always have to be in the bedroom and you'll want to utilize that skill set at work. This doesn't mean that you need to use a bedroom voice or eyes or imply that you're actually interested in being involved with a customer. This just means to take advantage of the subtleties of seduction and flirt with intention. Keep your goals in mind (customer enticement) and take advantage of the position of power you're in to direct conversation and interactions.

You're using your sex appeal to sell an experience, the bikini coffee experience to be more specific. It is expected of you to be flirty, outgoing, confident, sexy, and fun. Make sure to be all of those things and add shots of espresso without being too over the top in order to fulfill this expectation and play into every single one of your customers' fantasies.

Be the dream girl, oozing sex appeal both in your dress and manner.

## BARISTA NOTE

Sex appeal is one of the most powerful weapons in a bikini barista's arsenal and knowing how to use it to captivate the customer is not only expected but handled with confidence and seduction.

# LAW
# 18

MASTER THE 2 P'S: BE
PERSONABLE AND POSITIVE

*All I can control is myself and just keep having a
positive attitude.*

—Rose Namajunas

Your attitude will make or break your
success in the bikini coffee industry. There are no
exceptions to this rule. How to be positive and
professional while being mostly nude takes practice
but it is something you absolutely must master. A
bikini barista needs to be personable and positive in
order to attract (and keep) customers.

No one wants to listen to negativity, customers especially. They come to you to feel good and possibly escape the mundane of day to day life. Being negative could leave them with a bad taste in their mouth that even the sweetest coffee can't replace. Everyone has a personal life and personal problems, but being professional (even in a more lax work environment) needs to be the priority. Leave whatever might be on your mind at the door when you walk into the stand for your shift. Sometimes this is hard to do, but if you don't do it, your lack of professionalism will be noted. Few people want to listen to another's problems. Unfortunately, you're a captive audience and the dynamics of customer service in the bikini coffee industry means you are blessed to get to listen to theirs. Your frustrations might extend beyond your personal life, however, but it is never okay to express these to customers, whether it be about your boss, coworkers, or other customers. Especially not other customers. If a patron thinks you're bad mouthing someone else, they might get the impression that you'd do the same to them.

### *If You Don't Have Anything Nice To Say, Don't Say Anything At All*

While maintaining positive interactions is very important, you'll need to be personable for these interactions to even occur. Make sure that you are bubbly and fun. If you seem melancholy or under the weather, customers likely won't want to spend as much time with you. Your body language and inflection can say more than your words. Be mindful of this and carry yourself as if you're excited to be at work regardless of how your day/week is going. Check your posture and smile. Happiness is attractive and your goal as a bikini barista is to make yourself as appealing as possible. It can be very easy to go overboard with being fake happy. You'll need to balance positivity and realism. Don't be overly positive to the point of being obnoxious (yes, that's a thing). Instead, just be a slightly peppier version of yourself.

It's okay to add some sass, but keep it playful and lighthearted.

## BARISTA NOTE

Presentation and attitude play a pivotal role in customer service and mastering the 2 P's is an easy reminder of the their importance and the fact that you are in control of your energy and vibe.

# LAW
# 19

ACQUIRE REGULARS, ON THE
REGULAR

*Exceed your customer's expectations. If you do,*
*they'll come back over and over. Give them what*
*they want - and a little more.*

— Sam Walton

Making money (be it in the form of sales or
tips) is the ultimate goal for you and your employer.
You're at your job to make coffee and money.
Know how to do both by retaining customers and
increasing the number of regulars you have. This
will be safety net and soft guarantee when it comes

to how busy your shifts are (and how well you do in tips).

But what is a regular? A regular is a customer that is:

# **R**eliable
# **E**mpowering
# **G**enerous
# **U**nwavering
# **L**oyal
# **A**ppreciative
# **R**ewarding

Regulars can be a form of steadier income: they visit you day in and out faithfully. You can predict what time they'll come by and what they'll drink because it doesn't usually change. They are almost guaranteed income because of how "regular" they are in their visits to you. You can count on regulars to show up to your shifts, but this is earned and you'll need to continue to give the same amount of effort to retain them.

Getting regular customers can be as easy as being put on shifts at the same time every day (though this doesn't guarantee they'll continue to patronize the stand on your time), or as difficult as forging a relationship with a customer by "winning them over." If you're on your A-game and remember to ask the customer questions about themselves and remember the answers, you're off to a good start. Try to remember one detail about each customer you serve, then mention this the next time you see them. The more special you make them feel, the more loyal they will be to you. Once you start to see a customer with increasing frequency, challenge yourself to memorize their drink order or name (both is obviously the best). This will reinforce the idea that the customer matters to you and is significant.

Before any of this takes place, you'll need to show to the customers that you are consistent with your work ethic, attitude, and coffee. Humans are creatures of habit. Be smart and use that to your advantage when it comes to drawing in and retaining customers. The more consistent you are in all areas of your job, the more appealing you'll be as a bikini barista. If your mood is volatile and unpredictable, customers will be less inclined to stop by with any sort of frequency. Being late or calling out frequently will also damage the possibility of creating a regular customer base as they won't know when and where to find you. You could make amazing coffee one day and horrible coffee the next, which is also a huge deterrent. While the view is what attracts customers, good coffee will keep them coming back for more.

Once you've established a regular clientele, you must continue to be sociable, well dressed, on time, etc. If at any point you become unpredictable or inconsistent, the customer will likely shift their attention to another barista who is timely and cheerful. Remember that your regulars like you for a reason. Keep that same energy; keep the same customers.

## BARISTA NOTE

Acquiring regulars is essential to sustaining a business and growing a brand. They provide an unmatched level of loyalty and consistency that allows work to be enjoyable and most importantly, profitable.

# LAW
# 20

## TAKE THE GOOD AND THE BAD
## WITH A GRAIN OF SALT

*You have to take criticism with a grain of salt
because you're never going to please everybody.*

— Yolanda Adams

Bikini coffee isn't for the faint of heart or
mind. Toying the line between sex work and a
"civilian" job, the mental preparations that must be
taken before, during, and after work can make or
break a barista. Only the strongest can survive and
build a lasting and lengthy career as a bikini barista.

The public and private perception of bikini

baristas spans a broad chasm from devoted followers to disappointed friends and family. Understanding how to cope with this judgement will be integral to your success, making or breaking whether you can mentally handle this lucrative position. Slut shaming is rampant in society; be prepared to deal with this and answer questions as to why and how you could possibly do such a thing and respect yourself for it. Your family might not approve, thus hiding your profession from them might be necessary. While spinning a web of white lies to cover your tracks might be exhausting, it could be a self-preservation tool. Be wary of sharing any personal or identifying information when entering the industry if that's the case. Being outed can be embarrassing and stressful. Make peace and don't succumb to the stigma of working scantily clad. You should always be prepared to tell your family and friends what you do (even if that's not ideal) in order to handle the fallout that could occur afterwards.

If you feel shame in being a bikini barista, it probably isn't for you. It will eat you up over time and the industry will chew you up and spit you out. Constantly remind yourself why you chose this and be proud of yourself for doing something that not many girls could do. Never take any criticism personally. You *will* receive it but how you *perceive* it is on you. Haters will hate, but that doesn't mean you need to subscribe to it. Not allowing your self esteem to suffer because of the "morals" of others is vital to your survival and longevity as a bikini barista.

You'll play many roles in this position, ranging from barista to therapist. Customers love to talk about themselves, be it the good, the bad, and/or the ugly. Listening to customers vent or stress is emotional labor and you'll have to consistently provide this, day in and out, for dozens of customers a week.

Actively listening to customers isn't optional. Know how to appropriately respond to bad news such as deaths or cancer with sincerity. Not every conversation will be heavy, however. Celebrate births and promotions and birthdays with the same energy for everyone, regardless of how personally you know a customer. They'll appreciate it and will be more likely to continue patronizing the stand on your shifts. Aside from the extremes of being a captive audience and listening ear to your customers, you'll need to be prepared to make the same small talk over and over again. This in and of itself is a skill and can make your workday seem monotonous, dull, and eternal. Psych yourself up for this. Set yourself up for success.

Before your shift, you'll also need to get yourself in the right headspace to be mostly exposed to strangers. Some might say you respect yourself less for this. Modesty empowers some, while nudity empowers others. You need to know which it is for you, and if choosing to be a bikini barista, hopefully it's the latter. It will feel strange at first to wear little at work, but you'll be accustomed to this the longer you're in the industry. You'll find that your confidence and self-esteem/self-image will improve over time as well, due to constant compliments. Allow this, yet remain humble. Give yourself time to get comfortable, and you'll feel less overwhelmed. Exposure in this regard is daunting, and continuous male attention (and objectification) can be draining. Understand your limits and don't allow this to taint your view of men/your customers.

Being the recipient of constant male attention can have the positives of increased confidence as mentioned above, however, it can be detrimental to romantic relationships. Getting burnt out on compliments and attention, not to mention the constant sexualization, has the potential to make relationships seem less rewarding and personal. Leave the bikini barista at work in order to retain healthy relationships.

While checking in with yourself regularly to maintain your mental health is important, you'll need to know your limits in order to continue to give one hundred percent in the industry. It is easy to become exhausted due to the extensive preparation and emotional labor that is often overlooked when entering the industry. This can be a quick way to make money, but it isn't necessarily an easy way to make money. You will be the recipient of constant criticism and compliments. Take the bad with the good with a grain of salt and stay strong. You can and will succeed and you *are* cut out for this. Go get 'em, Tigress.

## BARISTA NOTE

Don't think for one second that being a bikini barista is all fun and games. If you don't have thick skin and the mental fortitude to handle criticism and stigma from family, friends, and strangers, it's best you become a regular barista.

# LAW
# 21

KNOW WHEN IT'S TIME TO PUT
DOWN THE PORTAFILTER AND
WALK AWAY

*The best time to start thinking about your retirement
is before the boss does.*

—Unknown

In this fast-paced and physically and
emotionally draining industry, it is important to set
longer-term goals in case of burn out. The bikini
coffee industry isn't for everyone and, unfortunately
many baristas have a shelf life. You will need to

check in with yourself frequently and regularly, as well as understanding your limits, otherwise, your performance could suffer, and cut your career as a bikini barista short. Have an exit plan while simultaneously pushing yourself for success. Use bikini coffee as a means to an end and set yourself up for success after your "retirement."

Depending on your personal goals, both for the short and long-term, this can look different for everyone. Are you going into bikini coffee to support yourself through school? Many baristas are.

Is this a side hustle?

Do you view bikini coffee as a quick way to make money? This is possible, but the income can make it difficult to leave, especially if you have become accustomed to a certain lifestyle. Working towards goals, however, is a great way to combat this. Be sure to share said goals with customers (if they ask). It will make you seem more driven and ambitious, which is an admirable trait to almost anyone. Regardless of how short or long-term the goals are, never lose sight of this. Instead, use it as a motivator and push yourself to be as successful as possible in the industry.

While bikini coffee will likely be temporary (be it several months to several years) it is crucial to prepare and anticipate for this. Have a plan for when you move on, be it to start a family or after completion of school. Hope for the best and prepare for the worst. As the longevity of your bikini coffee career is never guaranteed, this mindset will prove to be invaluable.

How your mental and emotional states of wellbeing are can also make or break your career. The industry is exhausting and burning out is not uncommon. Noticing one or more of several red flags could be indicative of needing to reconsider whether bikini coffee is right for you.

If your status as a bikini barista (which is not always well received) is negatively impacting your personal life or causing you to feel isolated and alone to the point of depression, it could be time to put down the portafilter. This could change over time as friends and family become more supportive, so sometimes patience is best in this case. You might find yourself losing patience and or feeling negatively towards customers. While there will always be a select few that rub you the wrong way, if you find yourself resentful towards customers more frequently than infrequently, consider taking a break or retiring. Your attitude could change for the worse which will only damage your sales and the likelihood of return visitors (the exact opposite of what you want to happen).

It is also a possibility that the pressure of maintaining competitive sales will lead to unnecessary and excessive anxiety. If you're dreading the idea of going to work for any reason at all (we all have bad days and weeks), don't continue to suffer. Your mental health and wellbeing is much more important than money. You can't buy sanity. You can, however, eliminate the stress of impending retirement from the industry by managing finances correctly and understanding when it is time to move on. Don't get stuck in a rut; plan for life beyond coffee and have an exit plan.

## BARISTA NOTE

Take advantage of your time and experience as a bikini barista, because it won't last forever. Take an honest assessment of your career goals and make sure you prepare for life after the portafilter.

# RECIPES

*When indecisive customers tell you to surprise them, it's good to be creative. It's even better to have a few suggestions ready to go that would appeal to anyone's taste. Every barista, bikini, or otherwise, should have a few "go-to" and popular drinks memorized and perfected.*

## SNICKERS MOCHA (16 oz.)

> 1.5 pumps Hershey's chocolate
> 1.5 pumps Caramel sauce
> 1 oz (3 second pour) Hazelnut Syrup
> 2 shots of espresso
> choice of milk

1. Start frothing the milk
2. Pull shots
3. Add ingredients to the cup
4. Top off with choice of milk and whipped cream

## SMOOTHIE (16 oz.)

> Jet Tea smoothie base
> ice

1. Add ice to the blender up to 16 oz mark
2. Add Jet Tea smoothie base until the ice is just beginning to float
3. Blend for at least 30 seconds or until smooth

## ALMOND JOY MOCHA (16 oz.)

        1 oz (3 second pour) Almond syrup
        1 oz (3 second pour) Coconut syrup
        1.5 pumps Hershey's chocolate
        2 shots of espresso
        choice of milk
1. Start frothing the milk
2. Pull shots
3. Add ingredients to the cup
4. Top off with choice of milk and whipped cream

## PINK PU$$Y RED BULL (24 oz.)

        2 oz (6 second pour) Pomegranate syrup
        2 oz (6 second pour) Passion Fruit syrup
        splash of orange juice
        1 can of Red Bull
        Ice
1. Add flavors to the cup
2. Add Red Bull
3. Stir, top off with ice

## BLENDED COFFEE BEVERAGE (16 oz.)

        2 shots cold espresso
        1.5-3 ounces of flavor (get creative)
        ice
        Soft serve base (or milk of choice)
1. Add flavor & shots to blender
2. Add ice to the 16 oz mark on the blender
3. Top off with soft serve base until the ice is just starting to float
4. Blend for 30 seconds or until smooth

## CARAMEL MACCHIATO (16 oz.)

    2 shots espresso
    choice of milk
    2.5 pumps Caramel sauce
    splash of Vanilla syrup

1. Start frothing the milk
2. Pull shots
3. Add ingredients to the cup
4. Top off with choice of milk and whipped cream

Note: If the customer orders their caramel macchiato "layered" add the ingredients in the following order and do NOT stir: vanilla, ice (omit if hot), milk, espresso, caramel.

## ITALIAN SODA (16 oz.)

    1.5 ounces (4.5 second pour) of flavor/syrup
    club soda
    splash of cream, OJ, lemonade (optional)
    ice

1. Add flavor to cup
2. Fill cup 2/3 full with ice
3. Top off with club soda & stir

## RED BULL ITALIAN SODA (24 oz.)

    1 can Red Bull
    approx 5 oz flavors (get creative)
    cream, OJ, lemonade (optional)
    ice

1. Add flavors to the cup (including cream, OJ, lemonade, etc.)
2. Add Red Bull
3. Stir, top off with ice

## CHAI LATTE (16 oz.)

    2.5 scoops Vanilla or Spiced chai mix
    choice of milk
    2 shots of espresso (but ONLY if it's "dirty")

1. Start frothing the milk
2. Add chai to the cup (pull shots if you're making the chai "dirty")
3. Top off with milk of choice

## WHITE ON WHITE MOCHA (16 oz.)

    2 shots white coffee
    2.5 scoops White chocolate
    choice of milk

1. Start frothing the milk
2. Pull shots
3. Add ingredients to the cup
4. Top off with choice of milk and whipped cream (optional)

## CARAMEL APPLE RED BULL (24 oz.)

    1 can of Red Bull
    2 pumps Caramel sauce
    2 oz (6 second pour) Green Apple syrup
    splash of cream
    ice

1. Add flavors & cream to the cup
2. Add Red Bull
3. Stir, top off with ice

## BLACK & WHITE MOCHA (16 oz.)

    2 shots espresso
    1.5 scoops White chocolate
    1.5 scoops Dark chocolate
    milk of choice

1. Start frothing the milk
2. Pull shots
3. Add ingredients to the cup
4. Top off with choice of milk and whipped cream

# BLACKBERRY CHEESECAKE RED BULL (24 oz.)

 2 oz (6 second pour) Blackberry syrup
 2 oz (6 second pour) Cheesecake syrup
 1 can of Red Bull
 splash of cream
 ice
1. Add flavors & cream to the cup
2. Add Red Bull
3. Stir, top off with ice

# GLOSSARY

## THE BIKINI BARISTA LANGUAGE

**BARISTA:** An individual well versed in the art of making espresso-based beverages.

**BIKINI BARISTA:** An individual well versed in the art of making espresso-based beverages but with a twist. These baristas wear bikinis and/or lingerie to work instead of traditional aprons or clothes.

**BIKINI COFFEE:** An umbrella term used to represent the overall bikini coffee industry and what it entails.

**BLENDED COFFEE BEVERAGE:** A milkshake-like beverage, but with the addition of espresso (usually cold shots). Often referred to by many of the following (trademarked/branded) terms: big train, frappe, frappuccino.

**BOXED SET (LINGERIE):** A set of lingerie that comes in a box. It's usually several cohesive pieces, color coordinated and always sexy.

**CAPPUCCINO:** A popular espresso-based beverage made with foamed milk. It can be wet (less foam) or dry (mostly foam).

**CUSTOMER:** The people that buy your coffee and tip you for your service; the more, the merrier.

**DECAF:** Decaf is short for decaffeinated espresso.

**ENERGY SPRITZER:** An iced beverage consisting of flavored syrup, any energy drink of choice (typically Red Bull), and ice with the occasional addition of juice or cream. It is often referred to as a spritzer, mimosa, or Red Bull Italian soda.

**ESPRESSO/COFFEE:** A delicious caffeinated beverage that can taste bitter and acidic if prepared incorrectly and carelessly.

**GRIND:** 1.How coarse or fine the coffee is made to be before extraction. 2.The act of working tirelessly day in and out to achieve excellence and success.

**HOPPER/GRINDER:** A container and machine that holds coffee beans and grinds them to perfection before the extraction process can occur.

**ITALIAN SODA:** A popular iced beverage consisting of seltzer, flavored syrup, sometimes with the addition of cream, orange juice, or lemonade.

**KNOCK BOX:** A box that you knock used espresso grounds into to remove them from the portafilter.

**LATTE:** A sometimes flavored espresso-based beverage made with steamed milk and espresso, having significantly less foam than a cappuccino.

**MACCHIATO:** Meaning "marked" in Italian; an espresso-based beverage where the espresso is added on top of the foam, "marking" it in the process.

**PORTAFILTER:** A removable component of the espresso machine that espresso grounds are added to and extracted from to make shots.

**REGULAR:** A (hopefully generous) customer who frequents you and your stand with loyalty and consistency.

**SEX APPEAL:** The quality of being attractive and alluring in a sexual way, whether directly or indirectly; a quality all bikini baristas must possess.

**SEX WORK:** A person who works in the sex industry (ex. stripping, escorting, selling "premium" content, producing porn, and possibly serving coffee mostly nude).

**SHOWS:** A euphemism for flashing a customer in exchange for a particularly generous tip. Keep in mind, that a show is not necessarily legal and not the industry norm.

**STEAM WAND:** A key part of the espresso machine that is used to froth and heat (steam) milk.

**TAMP:** The act of compacting espresso grounds before pouring using 20-30 pounds of pressure; the metal piece that enables you to do so.

**TIP:** A sum of money given on top of sale/service. Tips (also called gratuity) will (and should) be most of your income as a bikini barista.

**WHITE COFFEE:** Coffee that has been roasted for significantly less time than more traditional or darker roasts. Also has a higher caffeine content and a light and neutral nutty, flavor.

# INDEX

## M

## N

## O

## P

## Q

quality, 6, 9, 44, 45, 52

## R

recipes, 27
Red Bull, 58
regular (barista), 11, 55, 82
regular (customer), 17, 27, 47, 48, 57, 59, 60, 65, 74, 75, 76, 77

## S

safety, 22, 35, 37, 38, 44, 74
sales, 36, 47, 52, 56, 57, 58, 59, 74, 85
sex appeal, 4, 6, 54, 67, 70
sex work, 67, 78
shift(s), 6, 19, 31, 32, 33, 35, 36, 38, 39, 40, 45, 48, 52, 54, 55, 57, 58, 61, 66, 72, 75, 77, 80
shots, 8, 9, 28, 57, 58, 65, 70
slut shaming, 79
smoothie, 7
social media, 40, 41
spritzer, 7

## T

tamp, 7, 9
Twitter, 41

## W

Washington State, 3, 46, 50
white coffee, 7, 8, 9

www.ingramcontent.com/pod-product-compliance
Lightning Source LLC
Chambersburg PA
CBHW041711260326
41914CB00038B/1985/J